# WHITE WINE
# &
# MEDICAL MARIJUANA

Copyright © 2017 by Julia Cirignano. All rights reserved.

All rights reserved. This book or any portion thereof may not be reproduced or used in any manner whatsoever without the express written permission of the publisher except for the use of brief quotations in a book review or scholarly journal.

Front and Back Cover Illustration © 2017 Emily Surabian

Preface

*White Wine & Medical Marijuana* have been substances which have helped me ignore and balance out the topics I talk about within my poetry. Neither substance has necessarily helped me create great art, yet I feel that they help define me. If this title at all draws you in, I think we will get along.

This book of poetry is a compilation of poems about my life, sometimes involving the consequences of being high or intoxicated, yet the poems were created in moments of absolute sobriety.

I chose to title this book *White Wine & Medical Marijuana* because everything in the written word is never truly what it seems. While I put the enormous weight of this book's title on two flighty substances, I did so not in hopes of commemorating them but to draw in readers similar to me.

With this book of poetry, I hope to attract, startle, and also comfort you. I hope to surprise and indulge you, and leave you with a hint of hope no matter what pain and confusion may rest deep within you.

Enjoy,
-Julia Cirignano

**Rose Gardens**

I have galaxies and rose gardens in my head
They come out as whispers and rolled eyes
I blink, and a rose blooms but no one notices
I hum, and life is found on a new planet
A melody is created but they only see me walk
They see my curves but not my angles
They see my face but not my messy gardens
With roses and thorns and diamonds
That grow from the warm soil like new ideas

**Ghost**

I have a habit
Of drowning
It's nothing new
But I still hope
That someone
Will save me

**All of a Sudden**

You're shoving dry cheerios
Down your throat
For breakfast

Your hands are sticky
From the sugar
You're not a kid anymore

You're almost twenty years old
And you went to class this morning
Still drunk

**Sucker**

I
Want
You.
You
Want
Her.
But I'm still writing
In vertical lights
Wasting paper
On a man
Who warned me
Not to fall
In love with him.

## The Wolf

We're traveling down a snowy road together
You are eating me alive
Like the wild, majestic wolves
But I just smile
I gaze into their eyes
I pull you in
And remove your clothes

You've ripped out vital organs
I'm bleeding out
As we laugh and wrestle
And eat cereal together

I'm pale
All the blood has drained from my body
I feel sleepy, so I close my eyes
And rest my head on your chest

I wake up alone
Like a bad dream that followed me
Into reality
I see my open wounds gushing
I realize your eyes are yellow not brown

There are claw marks all over my body
Teeth marks
But I was the only one who didn't notice

## Without Blood I Can Fly

White marijuana smoke
Looks like milk
But tastes like knives
Cutting my throat
While easing the pain
Letting all of the blood
Flow out of my body

The bad is gone
So all that's left
Is the cream on the top
Light as a feather
Thick with satisfaction

## Suicidal Tendencies

It's easier to jump off the edge
If you're living on it

One slip will send you to your death
But the rush is exhilarating

Because even though you're close to death
You've never felt so alive

## I Pick Up My Mechanical Pencil

I spit-shine these words
Moist with my saliva
Licked by my split tongue

I write down words I have said
Words I wish I had said
And moments I have only imagined

I shave off a sliver of guilt
And follow my own foolish pleasure
Could it be genius?

I cling to a partial of pride
Left hanging off a cliff
And bring it back to solid ground

## Stale Urine

You thought it would be butterscotch kisses
But it turned out to be the smell of stale urine
In a public bathroom
The rusty stall doors are hard to manage
They're awkward, and you scrape yourself trying
You finally manage to escape, but
The mirror shows you what you've been
Running from
The dirtiest parts of your face
And the callused parts of your soul
Sand scratches your bare feet
Against the hot concrete
Sea salt stings the cracks in your cuticles
And your neck twitches when you try to stretch
The locks are worn off and broken
So you can't trust anything or anyone
Like you've never been safe
And you never will be

## 2 AM

I was ashing into my mother's plants on the front porch of our big yellow house with a pool and a dog and everything I would ever need when I realized that satisfaction is unattainable with a mind like mine.

**Spent**

The white t-shirt
That I used to
Pull over your head
And throw on the floor
Feels warm
Against your
Sweaty back
As you reach in
For a one-armed hug

**Mortal**

Life is just a bunch of moments
It's a beautiful flow
But then, we get sentimental about it

So dear, please stop
Being so damn nostalgic
About everything

It doesn't make you
A better artist
Or a better human being

**Fraud**

Weakness is strength
Vulnerability is essential
But I still
Walk into the bar
Oozing false confidence
And casual narcissism
So that they won't see

**Can't Help Myself**

You wear a do-rag
To achieve the perfect waves
In your hair

You drink a considerable
Amount of Ciroc
And Hennessy
Because you think
You quite possibly
Might be Drake

You have the most
Exquisite smile
And sly, seductive
Choice of words
You call me sweetheart
And boo

You have tattoos
Written in cursive letters
So I can't read them
But they still turn me on

I ask you what they mean
But I don't understand
Your explanation

You shave a delicate
Goatee and chin strap
Across your jaw
Smelling like

Spicy aftershave
And peppermint gum

It's no surprise

That the moment I saw you
All hope was gone

**Satisfaction**

The moment of relief
After I puke
Cold sweat
On the back of my neck
Hands hot
Heart beating
A long frizzy curl
Falling across my face

My face curves
Into a smile

## A Sensual Poem About an Unfortunate Affair

I like the way you drive your car up to me, casually rolling the window down. I like the way you tie your tie in my mirror and when you shower in my room in the morning. I like the way you roll over and encapsulate me in the middle of the night. I like when you call me and when you don't want to leave in the morning. Your skin feels thin under my fingertips as it floats over your bones and caresses your muscles. Your skin is dark brown. Your skin is warm and smooth. You say you're part Haitian and part Indian. I like the space your naked body takes up in my small bed. I wish you would be mine.

**Physical Therapy**

Your smile makes me giggle like a girl
And your hands make me moan like a woman

**Unsettled**

Never truly satisfied
Like a constant itch
*Almost* straight lines
*Almost* neat piles

Little mistakes
And imperfections
Build under my skin
So I scratch
Until little pieces
Of my body
Flake away

Slowly but surely
I rip through the many
Layers of irritation
Because sometimes
It's the little things
That eventually
Kill you

## Sexual Tension

I am
Flea-bitten
And
Philosophic
Gentle
And
Psychotic

You are
Simple
And
Demonic
Destructive
And
Idiotic

**The Beige Wall**

I don't know how many times
I've sat in silence behind that piano
Or I've belted out songs
At that plain beige wall
Because sometimes you need
An empty room
To feel full again

**Ambush**

My red lipstick is smooth and structured
My nails are cherry red and slick
My dress is black and see-through
My arms are tan and tight

But now my eyes feel heavy with makeup
My hair is sweaty and in a knot
My legs are weak; they shake
My nails are chipped and dirty
My lips are pale and pink
My dress is trapping me
My night is over

## "Oh Yeah, I Know Him!"

They all say
Because they all do
One way or another

You like to cat call
All of us
You like to send
Long texts
Declamations
Of your love

You like to have
Girls to bring
To family parties
To college parties

To show off
With no real intentions
Of commitment
And it hurts

It really fucking hurts
To be just another one
The next one
The last one
The current one
The side one
The main one

But at the end of the day
You told us

Who you were
So why are we all so surprised?

**Lucretius**

Ponders the connection between
A human's spirit and their body
And I'm interested
For a little while

But eventually I realize
It doesn't really matter
We're all excellent liars
And pretty losers
And well-meaning creepers

We all laugh and shit
And cry and reproduce
And it doesn't
Matter
If we have one spirit
Or an infinite amount

Because either way
We're bound to
Fuck it up

**Transparency**

Brains are more active
When filled with anxiety

So is the world more true
Or more cluttered
For the anxious?

**Debauchery**

We descend down the dirty hallways
Like geese heading south
We are trying to escape
The cold hours spent
Heads bent over books
Eyes bloodshot
By the illuminated light
Of the computer screen

We walk in a fashioned triangle
Pretending not to notice
Their eyes moving
Over our cool skin
Goosebumps appear
Stemming from their nasty thoughts

It's a rush to feel their attention
And a disgrace to like it so much

**War Zone**

Lipstick containers lined up like glossy
Black bullets
Little black dresses meant to burn your eyes
And steal your soul
The ticking of the clock and the beat of the music
Counts down the minutes until your death
Eye liner drawing out the rules
And the game plan
Eye shadow hiding our secrets
And romanticizing our pupils
Our heels make you gag and stare
Hallways and bright lights
Cold air and warm breath
You taste vodka on my tongue
Like I've poisoned you
But I've only poisoned myself
Sweat drips down my smile as I dance
My hair tangles itself around my neck
You can already see your victory
As if we are already in your room
But we're not and I'm gone
And I'm not even sorry
I'm running and laughing and broken
And I want to cry
But I keep running and laughing
And coughing on the cold air
My sweat freezes as it drips down
The back of my neck
I am trapped but I am running
So I will keep running
And pretend I am free

**Sunday Morning**

I'm hungover in an elevator
I imagine sticking my fingers in the door
But I don't

We're a caricature of a real relationship
And that's all we'll ever be
It's okay

You don't have to tell me you'll never leave
Just tell me you don't want to

**It Is What It Is**

Even if I'm too hot
I like a blanket over me

Sometimes I think
I'm like that with
Boys too

**Things Are Better This Way**

Cars rushed like fire-flies down the highway
We stood still with no envy of their rage
Oil from McDonald's fries covered my hands
I laughed so hard food fell out of my mouth
My throat burned with my smile
My face crunched and over heating
We were the only truck at the truck stop
I wished our doors could lock
The air outside my window cooled off my face
He gave me his jacket to sleep on
And asked if we could nap
I said no, but I let him drink my milkshake
He told me how his mom thought I took his virginity
And we laughed for a while about what she did
And didn't know
And then I told him to drive
Because I was about to give up
And ask for that nap
And he drove
Even though he was about to say yes
But it was better
This way

**Bitter**

Your slight limp
Makes me irritated
Because it forms
A nurturing feeling
In the pit of my stomach
And I'm trying to hate you

**Dm**

Music
Is
The
Sad
Man's
Sport

**Broken Paragraph**

He never cared about goosebumps or words.
I saw warm brown eyes
And a full white smile
I really didn't even care about him at all,
At first.
He played games on wax floors.
And he played games with me.

I lived moments that never really happened.
I saw people who weren't really there.
I felt feelings that he couldn't even imagine.
And all along I thought he was right next to me.
I thought he saw me.

But while I was watching him, he was watching them.
Their smiles like wax statues dripping in sweat.
Winged eyeliner romanticizing their souls.
I wear only goosebumps and anxiety.
My hands are sticky and my memories are all too clear.
They flow like dirty water from a rusted spigot
And they swarm around my head like nasty hornets.
They torture me but never you.

I want to shave my head
Because my hair keeps getting in my eyes.
And I blink so much that my eyes water.
I accidentally smear my makeup and my intentions.

I can feel each vein in my body.
I wish my heart would stop beating so loud
Because it's choking me.
My throat is closing and my mind feels small.
I can't stop thinking about you.
I can't think of another thought.
I'm so cold I wish I could dip myself
In the warmth of someone who understands.
But I'm shivering so much that I think I'm dying.
Goosebumps take over my entire body.
They encapsulate me in false empathy.
Goosebumps and words that he'll never understand.

## Help

It's squishing me
The need to see you
It makes my toes curl

It's consuming me
The need to see you
It makes my stomach hurt

**Weed is Supposed to Calm You Down But…**

My joint is almost gone
The ashes are sprinkled
Across the chipped paint
Of the windowsill

And
I think
About how
I could light
That boy on fire
Without even feeling
Bad

**Your Disease Was Contagious**

Once I met a person just like me
And accidentally feel in love with him

He turned out to be a psychopath
And he turned me into a psychopath

I wanted to shove him to the floor
Because he stopped loving me

What's wrong?
Do you think
I'm acting crazy?

## Straight Isn't the Only Right Angle

Sexuality is fluid
Everything is fluid
You see only straight angles
But there are loops and swirls
And twists that many deny

**A Sad Story**

There's something about the time in my life when I fell in love with you. It felt so good. I didn't know anything but I knew I wanted you. There was something so mysterious about you -- so exotic. I welcomed the danger you exuded. Although warning signs flashed right in front of me, I thought that as long as I had you, everything would be okay.

But that's the problem. Our relationship was all about possession. Possession mistaken for passion. But one day I woke up you were my entire world. My horrific, destructive, dominating, obsessive world that felt like one continuous rainy day. I had fallen in love with this life but there was a desperate, needy, dependency about the love we shared.

I resented you. I hated you for hurting me and also for becoming a person I needed; whom I thought I couldn't live without. I started to push and pull and grip onto you with white knuckles until our love slowly transformed into hate; a hot, sticky, hate that gulped for breath. Our love was a fire that my breaking heart was breathing life into. But I was angry at you and you were angry at the world.

We were at war which each other; testing each other and tearing each other apart piece by piece. Because I used to believe that passion equated to love.

**It's Not Funny**

This isn't like The Great Gatsby
He doesn't have parties
Waiting for her to show up
He has parties so
His whores can distract him
He doesn't hold the door for her
He slams it in her face
He doesn't kiss her on
Her Cinderella mouth
He slaps her ass because
His 'guys' told him to
And because
She
Laughs
It
Off

## A Song for Someone

Your once white teeth are now yellow. Your gums are blotchy. Your laugh is obnoxious. Your walk is awkward and you're shorter than I remember. You're skinnier now too, wearing your signature outfit: pajama pants and a white t-shirt.

You approach me, and your familiar scent makes me want to crawl into bed with you and also jump off a cliff. You act far too polite around me now, but sometimes you forget that you feel like you owe me the world. You slip up on the thin ice around us and insult me. We fall through the ice and doggy paddle through the thick silence that surrounds us.

We both want to rip off our skin — our external layers to reveal the trauma that still lingers with your touch, but we keep our composure. I force my lips to curve into a smile that shows both what I want you to believe and also what I want you to miss.

**Cheater**

Your sorry eyes
Won't get me this time
You won't *catch* me this time

Your sorry eyes
Can't fix it this time
You can't *save* me this time

Your lazy eyes
Tired from the other night
But
Mary
Jane
Can't
Save
You
This
Time

**I Like the Rain**

The smell of swelling wood
And wet grass
It makes me happy
Like everyone
Is on my level

But when the sun
Comes back out
My brain refuses
To recognize it

The rain is in my mind
It trickles down my neck
And there's a downpour
In my heart

The rain may pass
For some people
But for me
It has taken over
Every muscle in my body

I smolder in the sun
And I just burn
Burn and burn out

## The Girl with the Red Lipstick

Her red lipstick is painted onto her pale canvas
She doesn't wear any other make up
Her eyes are small and innocent
The sequins on her shirt remind me of Christmas
Every key she hits is perfect
A melody of delicate world winds
She is egotistic to no extreme
She undoubtedly doubts herself
Hearing the harmonies and not seeing the brilliance
The talent she inhabits
The talent that inhabits her
She reads off the notes
As they float through her mind
She is absolutely mistaken
Because she sees mistakes
That are not even there
She questions herself to the utmost degree
But all you see is a girl playing piano

**Ladies**

I've never been scared to break the rules
I've always been scared of unyielding order
Because they told me ladies don't start fires
So I lit a cigarette

Rules lie around waiting to be tested
Walls are only build up to be knocked down

I think ladies can drive pickup trucks
And ladies can swear in front of elders
I think that ladies can be naked or covered
All rules are only options created by cowards
Building walls to hold people back
Not to protect them

I've met ladies who are sarcastically polite
And ladies who wear the most mysterious smiles
But there is something similar
And unique behind each lady
No matter how polite you are
Or how casually narcissistic
You are a lady
And you are here to break the rules

**Cicatrix**

The spark
Between us
Still burns
Like a cigarette
Pushed deep
Into my
Wrist.

**Football Players**

I just want to lie in your bed
And pretend that we are in love
Because it makes my life bearable

I want to drink Captains with coke
On a Thursday night
Because it holds back the tears

I want you because you are warm blooded
So I guess we're both to blame

You've never lived a creative life
So you don't understand how unsettling it can be

Yet the idea of safety terrifies me
So maybe we are not meant to be together
Because you love normal and you don't believe in ghosts

You're confused by my confusion
And uneasy about the things I question
So I will just lie in your bed
Next to a warm-blooded boy
And you will hate me for my thoughts
And I will hate you for your lack of thoughts

But we will kiss
And I will stay

**Destructive**

Sometimes I need
My real girls
The ones who
R okay
Even excited
For the parties
With African
Men
And yayo

Sometimes
I need my girls
The ones who
Can roll blunts
Even with
Acrylic nails

The girls
With style
And sass
And attitude
And the girls
Who r okay
With smoky rooms
And big mattresses
And dirty bong water

Because sometimes
I just need
To have some
Unconventional fun

## My Dollar Store Wine Glass

The blur
Through my
Wine glass
Abstracts the
Truth
But I think
It's nice
To see a
Different
Perspective

**Moving On**

I drink this bottle
Of Captain Morgan
Determined and frantic
Like it is full of
The words you never said

Because sometimes
You have to forgive
The people who hurt you
Even if they never
Asked for your
Forgiveness

## A Realization That Came Too Late

You can't
Demand love
Just because
You think you
Deserve it

**Lost Kingdom**

One day
You will be drinking
And you will realize
That no amount of alcohol
Can erase me
And no amount
Of weed
Can make you feel
As mighty
As we were together

The world in our hands

Me in your arms

**You**

To avoid being
A caricature
Of yourself
You must always
Be evolving

Be who you are
In that moment
Not who you have been
Conditioned to be

Let yourself
Outgrow
Your old habits
And create new ones

Be ever changing
Expanding
Unfolding
Emerging
Into the world
Into *your* world

**I'm Tired**

Of arching my back
For a judge
With a British accent
Who doesn't see
It's the luck of the draw

She only sees
My lower leg swinging
And my incorrect diagonal
She thinks I could bend him in more
And lower my chin a bit

So she places me
6 out of 6
But that's okay
Because I don't care

**Love Gets Manipulated**

I want a love that's easy to remember
Easy to defend
A love that feels safe
Like coming home

**Victory**

One day I will be the thing I want to be
I'll lick the devil and tease an angel
I will have fangs and I will have claws
The sun will watch me set
And the ocean will watch me crash
I will smile when you say you hate me
I will question you when you say you love me

One day I will be the thing I want to be
I will have wings and I will have an army
I will get tequila wasted
And make a fool out of her
The hurricanes will watch me twirl
And strippers will watch me undress
And you will watch me *walk away*

**Fear of Mediocrity**

If I ever
Find myself
Living
An unsatisfactory life
I hope
I have
The guts
To change it

## The Moment You Lost Your Power

Was when I fell in love for the second time, and realized that you are not the only one who can give me that feeling. Not necessarily because of him, but because I now know that I have the freedom to pick the man I want — the opportunity to pick him better than I ever did before.

**Feeling Alive**

Roads are laid out for people to run down
And burn calories
And build muscle
We see dirt and hear birds
And appreciate it all

Paper is given to us
So we can make sense of the chaos
So we can feel a sense of calm
As the colors stick to the emptiness
And swirl into each other

We eat bright fruits
And feel the cool refreshing liquid
Drip down our elbows
The vitamins trickle down our throats
With sweet warmth and a sour hint

We hear *that* song in *that* spot
And we feel nostalgia
We call it coincidence
But nothing in this life is an accident
And our feelings are real

We should never feel bad
About being star struck by art
Or by nature or words
Or people or feelings or colors or fruit
We are human and we are flawed

Our sneakers imprint on the sand
Of the earth
And get washed away
But I guess
We have to be okay with that

**Freedom**

Oh, how much you can do as soon as you realize that you are free and you've been free all along. At any moment you can drop everything, people, plans, deadlines, schedules, sentimentality, or sadness. Sometimes familiar pain feels better than the unknown, but don't let that stop you. You can't give up on the world if you've only seem a small part of it. Travel, learn, explore, experience things, and take a step then a leap out of your dreary comfort zone. Because freedom is not handed to you — you have to fight for it.

## Acknowledgements

Select Poems - published in *The Endicott Review*
Select Poems - published in *The Endicott Review*
"Rose Gardens" - published in *The NY Literary Magazine*
"Rose Gardens" - published in *The Somerville Times*
"The Wolf" - published in *Red Wolf Journal*

www.ingramcontent.com/pod-product-compliance
Lightning Source LLC
Chambersburg PA
CBHW031429290426
44110CB00011B/584